PUZZLES ON THE BRAIN

Puzzicle #1, word for word: There is only one word in the English language that is *always* pronounced wrong. What is it?

Puzzicle #2 takes you a little deeper: It takes three men three days to dig three holes. How long does it take one man to dig half a hole?

Finally, a penny for your thoughts in Puzzicle #3: You have two coins that equal 35 cents. One is not a quarter. What are the coins?

Answers:

1. Whatever you say, the answer has to be *wrong*.
2. The question is full of holes, because there's no such thing as half a hole.
3. A quarter and a dime: one of them isn't a quarter, but the other one is.

Also by Alan Robbins:

PUZZICLES*
A CALL FOR MURDER*
CUT AND CONSTRUCT YOUR OWN
    BRONTOSAURUS*
ON THE TRAIN OF BLOOD
THE SECRET OF THE GOLD JAGUAR
GRANDMA'S PANTRY COOKBOOK (with
    Trudy Smoke)
MURDER IN A LOCKED BOX*

*Published by Ballantine Books

MORE PUZZICLES

Alan Robbins

BALLANTINE BOOKS • NEW YORK

Library of Congress Catalog Card Number: 88-92175

ISBN 0-345-35812-0

Printed in Canada

First Edition: April 1989
Second Printing: October 1989

A NEW SET OF CHALLENGES

Remember Puzzicles, those deceptively simple doodles that challenge your mind's Eye-Q? The ones you can't put down until you've found a solution?

Well, just when you thought you'd conquered your last one, and you could put your ingenuity to rest, along comes a complete new collection of tricky teasers.

Here again is a chance to dust off your mind, pump up your creativity, sharpen your pencil along with your wits, and get down to a good old-fashioned cerebral workout.

As with the first compilation of Puzzicles, many of the creative-thinking exercises herein have been based on other popular puzzles and puzzle types. The original sources for all of them would be impossible to trace. And while we don't claim to have invented any particular puzzle in this collection, we do wish to thank all those anonymous puzzlers who have passed along and improved upon these challenging diversions.

Let's begin with a few common matchstick Puzzicles, so called because they can be set up using actual matchsticks. (The diehard Puzzicler can solve them mentally, of course.) In this first example, see if you can rearrange all five lines above to show the number twelve.

2

In this matchstick Puzzicle, arrange all six lines to make three and a half dozen.

Sorry about that last one, but while we're on the subject, can you rearrange these four lines to show one thousand?

4

Move exactly three of the lines above to leave exactly one
—no more, no less.

Here's another common type of matchstick Puzzicle using boxes. Can you remove only two lines from the above image so that you end up with exactly two squares?

And finally, for the moment at least, move exactly four of the lines above to show ten squares.

ARMY
DINE
TEAK
HURT
SAIL

Another common form of Puzzicle uses words. Here are some easy word Puzzicles to loosen you up. First, what do all the words above have in common?

8

TON
PET
ROT

The same common three-letter word could be placed in front of each of the words above to form a new word. What is the three-letter word?

BCE
IOP
TUY

What do the nine letters above have in common?

LLPN
SSSS
EEEE

A common English word can be made using the letters you see here. What is it?

QWERTY UIOP

No doubt you recognize the letters above from the top row of a typewriter. A common English word that you most certainly saw today can be made using seven of the letters, with repeats. What is the word?

_EE _EE
_OO _OO
_SS _SS

How about filling in the blanks on these common words?

HIJKLMNO

The letters above represent a common household substance. What is it?

ABCDEFG
HIJKMNO
PQRSTUV
WXYZ

And lastly, here's an idea for a greeting card Puzzicle. On what holiday would you send the above alphabet?

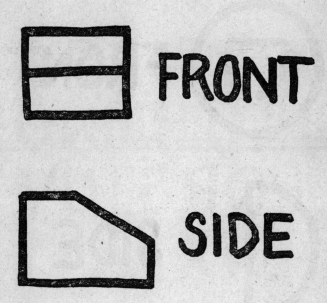

FRONT

SIDE

Here are a few shape Puzzicles to test your Eye-Q. The images above show the front and side views of an object. What would the object look like in 3-D?

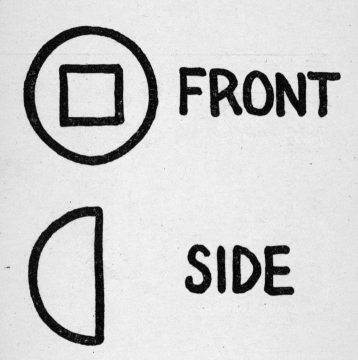

FRONT

SIDE

Here, again, are the front and side views of an object, leaving you to determine the 3-D view.

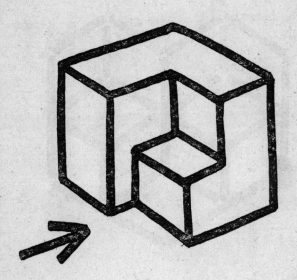

In the above object, what would the side view, from the direction of the arrow, look like?

The lines here show two completed cubes in perspective. What is the least number of lines you'd have to add to create a third cube?

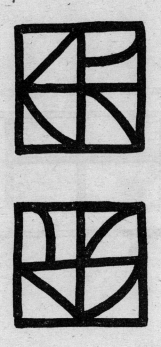

Is the image above the same as the one below—but turned?

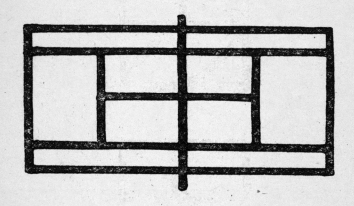

This image shows something very familiar. Can you tell what it is?

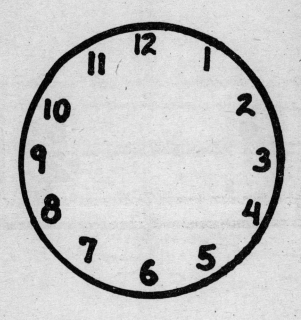

Can you divide this clock face in half with a straight line so that the sums of the numbers in each half are equal?

22

Presenting the world's simplest connect-the-dots Puzzicle.
Just connect the dots with the longest line possible.

Four straight lines added to these circles will produce a common household expression. What is it?

Here's a dot Puzzicle (or Dotticle) to drive you to distraction. Can you arrange the ten dots above into five rows with three dots in each row?

ABCDEF GHIJKLMNO PRSTUVWXY

Another alphabetic greeting card. On what inventor's birthday would you send the above alphabet?

2 4 8 10
20 22 __

Now that you're on your guard, let's try some series Puzzicles for a change. What is the next number in the above series?

$$\frac{\quad 10 \quad 11}{21 \quad 31 \quad 401}$$

In this case, find the first number in the series.

1 2 3 2

1 2 3 4

2 1 2 _

How about filling in the blank in this logical series?

PRND__

What are the next two entries in this familiar sequence. (It really is, trust us.)

12 13 _ 23

And here's another familiar sequence of numbers. Can you fill in the blank?

2 1 2 2 2
1 2 2 2 1

The numbers above represent the digits one to ten, in order, according to a code. Can you figure out what it is?

$$101-102=1$$

Here are a few Puzzicles that use equations to test your mettle (if not your math). For example, can you make the above equation correct by altering the position of only one digit?

$$340 = 1$$

What simple operation can you perform on the above equation to make it correct?

$$5+5=2$$

This equation is actually correct just the way it is. How can that be?

1-60=23

This equation, too, is correct just the way it is. What does it represent?

$$5+5+5=550$$

All you have to do here is add a single line to the equation to make it correct. The answer does not involve altering the equals sign.

If there are twelve three-cent stamps in a dozen, how many twenty-five-cent stamps are there in two dozen?

Now listen carefully to this one because it's tricky. One train leaves station A at 8AM going 35 mph. Another train leaves station B at 9AM going 40 mph. Which train will be closer to station A when they meet?

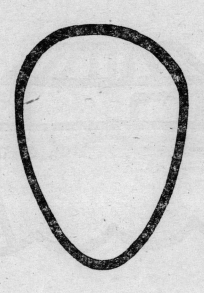

Here's a cooking Puzzicle. If one egg boils in three minutes, how long would it take to boil six eggs?

There were fifty pairs of two-legged beasts and twice as many pairs of four-legged beasts. So how many beasts in all did Moses put on the ark?

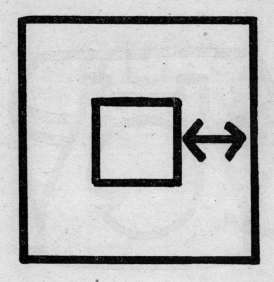

The image above shows a raft in the middle of a pool. The distance between the raft and the side of the pool (shown by the arrow) is ten feet all around. How can you place two 9½ foot long planks of wood (without any other tools) so you can get to the raft without swimming?

42

If one-tenth of the people in town have unlisted phone
numbers, and you pick one thousand names at random
from the phone book, how many of the ones you picked
will have unlisted numbers?

A woman has only three children, but half of the children are boys. How is that possible?

Let's make up for that last one with another, in the same vein. This woman has given birth to two sons, born at the same time and identical-looking. But she has never given birth to twins. How is this possible?

And finally, another old standard, reborn as a Puzzicle. Three cannibals and three missionaries must get across the river. Their boat holds only two at a time, but the cannibals on shore can never outnumber the missionaries. What's the quickest way to get everyone across?

46

More matchsticks. Can you remove exactly three lines from the above image to leave exactly three triangles, no more or less?

Here are twenty-four lines showing nine equal-size squares. Can you remove exactly eight lines and leave exactly two squares?

48

In this one, there are eight equal-size triangles. Remove four lines and leave exactly four triangles.

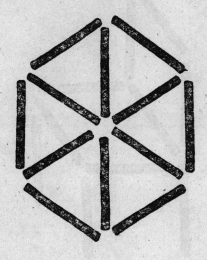

The lines above form six small triangles. What are the fewest number of lines you would have to move to create six squares instead?

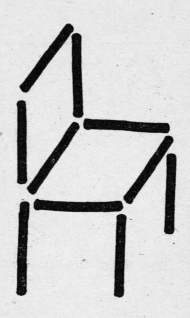

Here you see a chair, facing to the right, composed of ten lines. What are the fewest number of lines that must be moved so that the chair will be facing in the opposite direction?

In three moves can you transform this house into a pair of glasses?

VERMONT
VIRGINIA
TENNESSEE
NEW YORK
CONNECTICUT
KENTUCKY

A few more word Puzzicles for your enjoyment (we hope).
What do all the above states have in common?

FINEST
AVAIL
TENAM
DRIVERS

What do all these words have in common?

RRT
MLY
LBM

Here are three place names that all have the same letter missing. Can you add the letter to each of them and spell out the names?

OOKKEE

Believe it or not, the unusual sequence of letters you see here is found, in the same order, in a common English word. What is the word?

EADPRS

The letters above can be rearranged to spell six common words in English. What are they?

A B D O
P Q R

The seven letters you see here have a characteristic in common, not shared by the other letters of the alphabet. What is it?

I

What English word, printed in capitals, reads the same forward, backward, and upside down? We've given you the obvious answer above, but there's another one.

One above and another in *how*, two in *wow*, and three in *bowwow*; so how many *W*s are there in all?

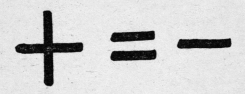

What word is made shorter by adding one syllable to it?

IT WAS AND I SAID NOT BUT

Can you punctuate the sentence above so that it makes sense? The answer is yes, but how would you do it?

WIG
SIN
BOG
MAN

What three-letter combination can you add to the end of each of these words to create four new words?

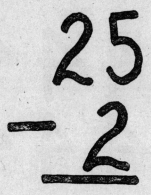

Back to some math Puzzicles (they're the ones that call on as little math as possible). How many times can you subtract the number 2 from the number 25?

4 4 4 4
4 4 4 4

There's an easy way to arrange eight fours so that they illustrate the number 500. How would you do it?

9999

How about arranging the four nines you see here so they show the number 100?

100

0

1000

I

100

And finally, a real challenge. The numbers above, read from top to bottom, represent a type of book you undoubtedly read as a child. What is it?

Here's a second round of Puzzicles that call on your sense of shape. Shown above are three different views of the same diamond, which is turning on its axis like a planet. Only four of its eight sides are visible in each view. What pattern is on the side in question?

Like the last one, these images show three different views of the same object, in this case a box with the front end open. Which way should the arrow be pointing in the third view?

Here's a deceptively simple one for the deceptively simple-minded. Which way should the lines be going on the above folded piece of lined paper?

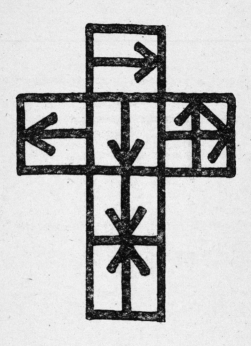

That last one was so simple, we'll compensate for it with this one. If you were to fold the above into a cube, how many times on the completed cube would arrows be pointing toward each other across an edge?

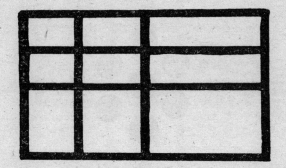

How many times does a rectangle appear on this page?

The above pattern should be familiar to you, since it appears on something you've often used. We'll start off by telling you it isn't on a telephone. Where does it appear?

And here's another image you've often seen. We'll even give you a hint and tell you that it represents a hole. Where have you seen this shape?

Although their solutions involve cutting, it's better if you solve these scissor Puzzicles mentally. (After all, a sharp pair of scissors is still duller than a sharp wit.) First of all, can you rearrange these four shapes to form an identical fifth one?

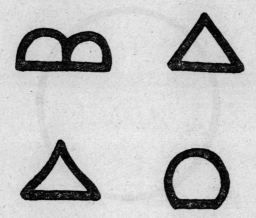

What familiar set of objects do the above shapes represent?

How would you divide the above circle into eight equal pieces if you could only do it with three straight cuts?

Can you cut the above shape into four parts that are themselves identical in size and shape to each other and identical in shape to the whole?

It's hard to believe, but there is a way to make two straight cuts in the above shape, so that the three resulting pieces can be rearranged to form a perfect square. How would you make the cuts?

Two straight cuts in the above shape will also divide it into three pieces that can be rearranged to form a square. Where would you make the cuts?

How about arranging these four shapes to show a perfect cross?

TTFFSS_

What letter comes next in the above series?

DEER
DOG
CAT
WOLF
RAT

What word above doesn't belong with the others?

02234
21201

Here are the digits 0 to 9 in order, represented by a very
simple code. Can you tell how the numbers above relate to
the digits?

1 2 6 10

These numbers have a common characteristic that is not shared by any other numbers in between. What is it?

H I O X
Z S N

The above letters all have one thing in common. What is it?

JQKA_

Last series Puzzicle for this collection. What comes next?

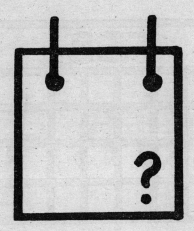

Listen carefully to this one. The day before the day after tomorrow will be Saturday. The day after the day before yesterday was Thursday. What day is today?

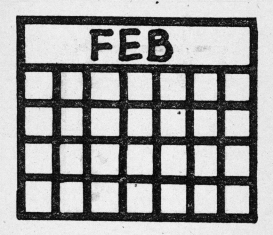

Here's another one that tests some basic calendar knowledge that no one seems to have. How many times in four years does a month with twenty-eight days occur?

One April Fools' Day, you go to sleep at 9 o'clock at night, having wound up and set your alarm clock to wake you at 10 AM. If you sleep until awakened by the alarm, how many hours of sleep will you get?

Another problem requiring logic (or at least that peculiar form of logic that Puzzicles seem to require). The plane had 100 people on board, three times as many passengers as crew. When it crashed, half the crew and twice as many passengers were killed. So how many survivors in all were killed in the crash?

And now for a few mystery Puzzicles. The murderer left through the only front door at exactly two o'clock. The detective entered through the same front door at exactly two o'clock. Yet the detective didn't arrest the murderer. Why?

To prevent a coup by the children of the officers, the general passed a law that any boy whose father was in the military was to be shot. How did the general's own son avoid that fate?

Two men were dueling. Both their bullets hit their mark, but neither one was injured. How is that possible?

The wishing well will grant your wish if you first perform one simple task. Fill the bucket with water from the well but don't take any water from the well. How do you do it?

This one's perhaps one of the best known Puzzicles, but we'll try it out on you anyway. An explorer sees a bear 100 yards due south of him. The bear walks 100 yards due east while the explorer stands still, at which point the explorer fires his rifle due south and kills the bear. Now, what color is the bear?

Question: Can you drop a raw egg twelve feet without breaking its shell? The answer is yes, but how?

How could two people divide a pie to ensure that they would get equal portions, if only one was allowed to do the cutting? There's a very neat solution to this.

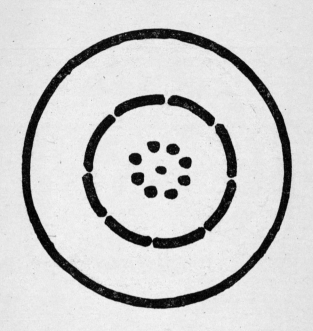

This one too has a very intriguing solution, which also happens to be true. Why are manhole covers round?

A philosopher, too busy contemplating the stars, fell into a cistern (a well in which water diverted from a nearby river is stored). He is one foot beyond the only length of rope in the village. How did the simple handmaid get him out?

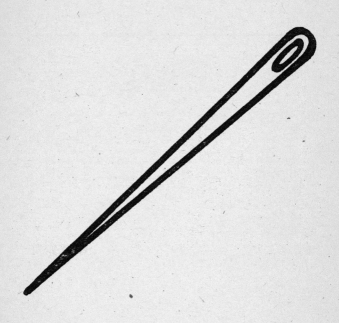

We've saved one of the cleverest riddle Puzzicles for last, to keep you happy until the next volume. Here it is. There is one simple, unfailing way to find a needle in a haystack. What is it?

ANSWERS

1.

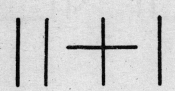

2. Like we said, three—and a half dozen.

3. The letter *M* represents 1,000 in Roman numerals.

4.

5. (The small square in the upper right and the large square that contains it.)

6. (The two large squares and the eight small squares within them.)

7. Each can be rearranged to spell a woman's name: *Mary, Enid, Kate, Ruth, Lisa.*

8. The word *car* can be added to each one to create *carton, carpet,* and *carrot.*

9. The plural of each letter creates a sound-alike for a real word: *bees, seas, ease, eyes, owes, peas, teas, use,* and *wise.*

10. The word is *sleeplessness.*

11. The word is *typewriter,* which appears in the question. Other ones can also be made, such as *propriety.*

12. *Teepee, voodoo, assess.*

13. The answer is *water.* Why? Because the letters shown are H-to-O, or H_2O.

14. Christmas, of course. There's no L. (Noel).

15.

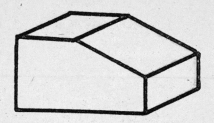

16.

17.

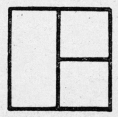

18. None. Just turn the image upside down, and you'll see three cubes.

19. It sure is.

20. It's a tennis court, seen from directly above.

21.

22.

23.

24. Like so. We didn't say the rows had to be parallel.

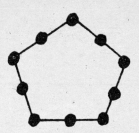

25. Alexander Graham Bell. It's the alphabet as it appears on a telephone dial. No Q or Z.

26. The next number in the series is 44. The numbers are generated by alternating between *adding* to the previous number and *multiplying* the previous number by 2.

27. The first number is 0. Add the digits in each number in the series, and you'll see why.

28. Give yourself a pat on the back if you got this one. The numbers in the series represent the number of characters in the Roman numerals 1 to 12: I, II, III and so on down to XII, which has three characters (one X and two I's). So the answer is 3.

29. The next two entries are 1 and 2. This series shows the gears on an automatic transmission: park, reverse, neutral, drive, 1 and 2.

30. Sorry about this one. The answer is *U*. You now, no doubt, recognize this series as a section of the channels on an ordinary TV dial.

31. These numbers show the number of vowels in each of the words from one to ten.

32.

$$101 - 10^2 = 1$$

33. Just turn the page upside down!

34. Simple. Five fingers plus five fingers equals two hands.

35. Also simple. One day minus sixty minutes equals twenty-three hours.

36.

$$5 + 5 \overset{\downarrow}{4} 5 = 550$$

37. Twenty-four. No matter how much the stamps cost, there will always be twelve in a dozen.

38. Neither will be closer to station A when they meet, because when they meet, they'll be at the exact same point.

39. It will still take three minutes, assuming you boil them all together in the same pot.

40. None. Moses didn't put any beasts on the ark; Noah did.

41.

42. None. People with unlisted phone numbers aren't listed in the phone book.

43. Because the woman has three boys. Half of each child might be a boy, but so is the other half. (Don't groan. We never said Puzzicles were educational.)

44. The two boys are part of a set of triplets.

45. Swim.

46.

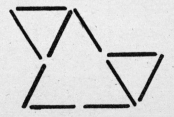

47.

48.

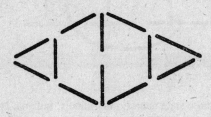

49. You don't have to move any of the lines. Just think of the image as a transparent cube seen from one corner. The six sides of the cube are the six squares.

50. You can do it in two moves. The resulting chair will be upside down.

51. Like so, to create a pair of wine glasses, not spectacles.

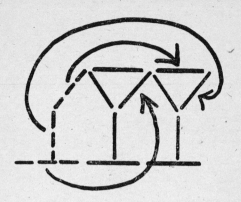

52. All these state names, plus Illinois, Indiana, North Carolina, and Pennsylvania appear on a Monopoly board.

53. The addition of a single space to each of them gives them meaning: FINE ST, AVA IL, TEN AM, DR IVERS.

54. The letter *A* added to each set of letters creates a familiar place name: *Ararat, Malaya, Alabama.*

55. *Bookkeeper.*

56. *Drapes, rasped, spader, parsed, spared,* and *spread.*

57. They each contain inner spaces like the triangle in *A* and the two loops in *B*.

58. *NOON*.

59. None. There are no *W*s in the word *all*.

60. *Short*. Add the syllable *er* to it and you have *shorter*.

61. It was *and*, I said, not *but*.

62. Try *gle* to create *wiggle*, *single*, *boggle*, and *mangle*.

63. You can only do it once. After you subtract 2 the first time, you'll be subtracting it from 23, then from 21, and so on.

64.

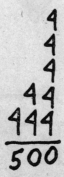

65.

99 9/9

66. The numbers represent the word *comic*, as in comic book. 100 is *C* in Roman numerals; zero is used as the letter *O*; 1000 is *M*; the *I* is used as itself; and the 100 is another *C*.

67.

68.

69.

70. Two times. Try folding it if you don't believe us.

71. The answer is 37. Did you remember to count the word *rectangle*, which is also a rectangle that appears on the page?

72. The pattern shows the holes on a can of kitchen cleanser.

73. It's the hole on an audio cassette.

74. Just push them together to create a fifth one in the empty space.

75. They are the top segments of the four suits: heart, diamond, spade, and club.

76. First, cut it in half to make two pieces. Stack those two pieces and cut them in half again, to make four pieces. Finally, stack the four pieces and cut in half again to make eight equal pieces.

77.

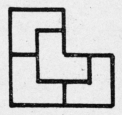

78.

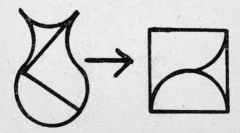

79.

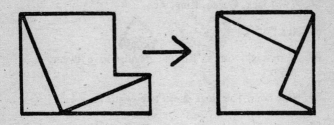

80. Arrange the shapes to show the shadows behind the cross.

81. *E* comes next. The series shows the first letter in the name of each digit starting with *two*.

82. The word *cat* doesn't belong, since it's the only one that doesn't create a new word when reversed.

83. They show the number of loose ends in each digit: zero, a closed circle, has none; one, a straight line, has two; and so on.

84. Each of their names is composed of three letters.

85. They all read the same upside down.

86. *Two*. Jack, Queen, King, Ace . . .

87. It's Friday.

88. Forty-eight times. All the months have twenty-eight days.

89. One hour. The clock doesn't know it's ten PM.

90. None. There were no survivors killed in the crash; that's why they were survivors.

91. Because one went out at 2 AM, and the other entered at 2 PM.

92. The general was a woman.

93. They weren't dueling with each other.

94. If you just lower the bucket into the water and let it sit there, you'll fulfill both requirements of the task.

95. The only way the explorer could follow the movement of the bear, and still be pointing due south would be if he were standing at the North Pole. Therefore the bear must be white. It's a polar bear.

96. Drop the egg from fifteen feet. The shell will break, of course, but it *did* fall twelve feet without breaking.

97. Have one person cut the portions and the other one choose which one he wants. Think about it. The one who cuts is forced to be fair.

98. So the lids, which are heavy, can't fall through the opening. If the lids were square, they could always fall through diagonally. But on a round lid, the diameter is always the same . . . wider than the opening!

99. By diverting more water into the cistern, raising the water level, *and* the philospher, high enough to reach the rope.

100. Set the haystack on fire. When it all burns down to ash, just blow it away and you'll have your needle. Who says Puzzicles can't solve the world's greatest problems?

ABOUT THE AUTHOR

More Puzzicles is the second volume in ALAN ROBBINS'
series of Puzzicles mind games for Ballantine Books. Mr.
Robbins is an award-winning graphic designer and writer. His
other books include *Cut and Construct Your Own Bronto-
saurus* and the interactive mystery novels *A Call for Murder*
and *Murder in a Locked Box*.